Unto Us A SAVIOR IS BORN

Story and Coloring Book

Mackenzie J. Wallace

Cover designed by Mahmud Didar
Interior Illustration by Omar Faruq Rijbi

PureBlue Publications
www.purebluepublications.com
purebluepublications@gmail.com

Copyright
Copyright © 2024 by PureBlue Publications
Printed in the United States of America
All rights reserved.

Scripture references are taken from the Holy Bible,
King James Version

This precious gift belongs to:

_____

During King Herod's reign, there lived a kind man named Zacharias. He was a priest who obeyed God. He and his wife, Elisabeth, had no children because his wife could not get pregnant, and now, they were both very old.

Reference: Luke 1:5-7

One day, while Zacharias was performing his priestly duties in the Lord's temple, an angel named Gabriel appeared to him. Zacharias was afraid! The angel told Zacharias, "Do not be afraid, Zacharias! God has heard your prayers."

Reference: Luke 1:11-13

The angel also told Zacharias that his wife would have a son named "John" who should not drink wine or other strong drinks. He will be filled with the Holy Spirit and help many people turn to God.

Reference: Luke 1:13-17

Zacharias did not believe the angel's words and asked, "How could this happen?"

Reference: Luke 1:18

The angel told him that because of his doubt, he would not be able to speak until John was born.

Reference: Luke 1:19-20

Meanwhile, people were outside the temple praying and waiting for Zacharias to return to minister to them. They wondered, "Why is Zacharias delayed so long in the temple?" When Zacharias finally returned, the people were astonished that Zacharias could not speak. He made gestures with his hands but remained speechless.

Reference: Luke 1:10, 21, 22

Afterwards, God then sent Gabriel to visit a young lady named Mary, who was engaged to marry Joseph. Gabriel told her, "Rejoice, highly favored one, the Lord is with you: you are blessed among women!"

Reference: Luke 1:27, 28

Mary was a little troubled by the meaning of the greeting. "Do not be afraid, Mary," said the angel, "You shall become pregnant by the power of the Holy Spirit and have a Son, and you shall call Him, "Jesus." He is the Son of God."

Reference: Luke 1:29-35

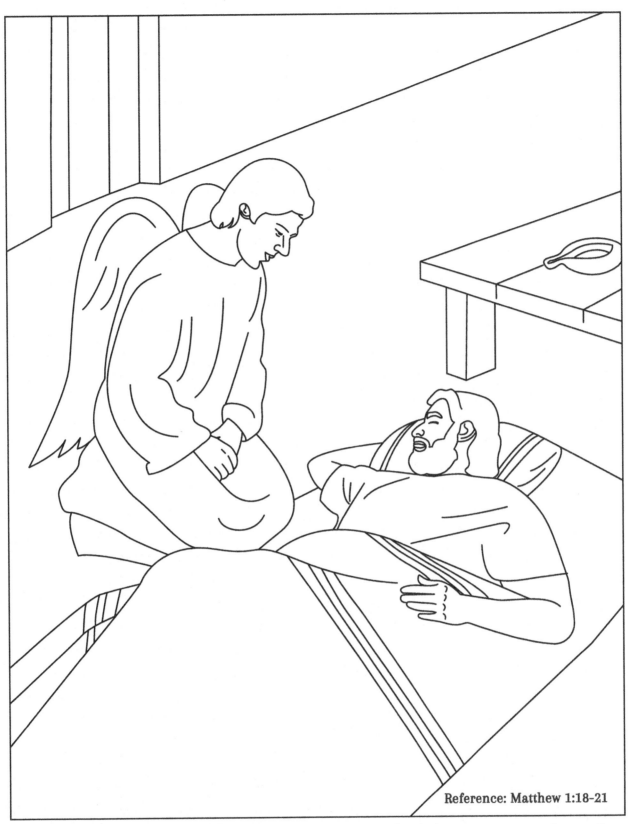

Reference: Matthew 1:18-21

Joseph received the news and thought that Mary had done an immoral act. But while Joseph reasoned to put her away privately, he drifted to sleep, and an angel came to him in a dream. The angel said, "Joseph, son of David, do not be afraid to take Mary as your wife. She became pregnant by the power of the Holy Spirit. She shall, therefore, have a son, and you shall call Him Jesus because He shall save His people from their sins."

Mary was overwhelmed with joy!

Mary was then told the wonderful news that her cousin, Elisabeth, was also pregnant, so she left eagerly for Elisabeth's home.

Reference: Luke 1:36-39

Soon enough, Mary arrived at Elisabeth's home. When Elisabeth heard Mary's voice, the baby leaped into her womb, and Elisabeth was filled with the Holy Spirit.

Reference: Luke 1:40, 41

Finally, after nine months, Zacharias' and Elisabeth's baby arrived. Many family members and neighbors visited the couple to celebrate the new birth.

Reference: Luke 1:57, 58

Still unable to speak, Zacharias requested a writing pad and wrote the baby's name: John. Their friends marveled at the name because no one in their family was called John. Immediately, Zacharias was able to speak. He was thrilled and praised God. Everyone was quite amazed!

Reference: Luke 1:58-66

Months later, a decree required everyone to be taxed; as such, Joseph and Mary traveled to Bethlehem because Joseph was from David's lineage. Mary was now at the late stage of her pregnancy, so it was almost time for baby Jesus to arrive!

Reference: Luke 2:1-5

After hours of traveling, David and Mary finally arrived in Bethlehem, but all the inns were occupied. Thankfully, however, someone offered them a stable. There, the Son of God was born!

Reference: Luke 2:5-7

Meanwhile, not far away, three shepherds were in a field watching their sheep during the night.

Reference: Luke 2:8

Suddenly, an angel appeared with great light shining around them. The angel said, "Do not be afraid! I am bringing the good news of great joy! A Savior, Christ the Lord, was born this day in Bethlehem. You will find the baby wrapped and lying in a manger."

Reference: Luke 2:9-12

Suddenly, a multitude of angels praised God, singing, "Glory to God in the highest, and on Earth peace, goodwill toward men!"

Reference: Luke 2:12-14

When the angels left, the shepherds traveled hastily to the town of Bethlehem and found Mary, Joseph, and the baby lying in a manger.

Reference: Luke 2:15, 16

The shepherds left, glorifying and praising God. They told everyone they met about what they saw and heard regarding the child, Jesus.

Reference: Luke 2:17-20

Sometime after, there were three wise men from the East who saw the star, foretold in the prophecy, so they traveled to Jerusalem and asked, "Where is the King of the Jews? We have seen His star in the East and have come to worship Him."

Reference: Matthew 2:1, 2

They were brought before King Herod. When the king heard the news, he was troubled.

Reference: Matthew 2:3

He gathered all the Jewish priests and teachers and demanded that they should tell him where Christ should be born. They answered, "Bethlehem!"

Reference: Matthew 2:4-6

King Herod spoke secretly to the wise men, telling them to go and search diligently for the child in Bethlehem. And when they have found Him, they should tell him so he, too, may come and worship the King.

Reference: Matthew 2:7, 8

After the wise men left King Herod's presence, the star appeared, which they saw in the East.

Reference: Matthew 2:9, 10

The star led them to Bethlehem and hung over the young child.

Reference: Matthew 2:9

When they saw the young child with Mary, his mother, they bowed down and worshipped Him, giving Him gifts such as gold, frankincense, and myrrh.

Reference: Matthew 2:11

Reference: Matthew 2:11

In a dream, God warned the wise men that they should not return to King Herod but, rather, travel another way to their home.

Reference: Matthew 2:12

Reference: Matthew 2:12

The angel of the Lord also told Joseph, in a dream, to flee to Egypt and stay there until he was told when to return because Herod would look diligently for the child to destroy Him. Joseph arose during the night, took Mary and the young child, and left for Egypt.

Reference: Matthew 2:13-15

A long time ago, our first parents sinned, and as a result, death was brought to our world. Romans 6:23 tells us, "For the wages of sin is death," but God loves us so much and is not willing for any of us to perish; so, He sent His only begotten Son as a **gift** to redeem us from sin. God desires to give us the *gift* of eternal life through Jesus Christ, our Savior. He is the ultimate gift to all the world.

We share our gifts with those who are in need!

We share our gifts with those who are lonely!

Our Heavenly Father sent His Son, Jesus Christ, to preach the good news of salvation, heal the broken heart, release those in the bondage of sin, and minister to those in need so that through Him, we might be saved.

It is by grace we are saved through faith and not our own works; salvation is the gift of God through Jesus Christ

Reference: Isaiah 61:1, 2; Ephesians 2:8.

ANGEL

SHEPHERD

SHEEP

WISE MAN

KING

CAMEL

STAR

JOSEPH

MARY

BABY

Thank you

Your order made our day! We hope we make yours.

We are thrilled to share this experience with you, and we hope that your child will find it enjoyable. Please do not hesitate to explore more books from our collection.

If you have any questions, contact us anytime. We'd love to hear from you.

 purebluepublications@gmail.com

Made in the USA
Middletown, DE
18 March 2024